I0428824

U.S. ENVIRONMENTAL PROTECTION AGENCY

OFFICE OF INSPECTOR GENERAL

# Examination of Costs Claimed Under EPA Cooperative Agreements CB-97324701 Through CB-97324705 Awarded to Alliance for the Chesapeake Bay, Inc.

Report No. 12-4-0720                  August 22, 2012

**Report Contributors:**    Jean Bloom
Edward Rivers
Shannon Schofield
Richard Valliere

## Abbreviations

| | |
|---|---|
| CA | Cooperative agreement |
| CFR | Code of Federal Regulations |
| EPA | U.S. Environmental Protection Agency |
| OIG | Office of Inspector General |
| Recipient | Alliance for the Chesapeake Bay, Inc. |

# Hotline

**To report fraud, waste, or abuse, contact us through one of the following methods:**

**e-mail:** OIG_Hotline@epa.gov                 **write:** EPA Inspector General Hotline
**phone:** 1-888-546-8740                                     1200 Pennsylvania Avenue NW
**fax:** 202-566-2599                                            Mailcode 2431T
**online:** http://www.epa.gov/oig/hotline.htm        Washington, DC 20460

**U.S. Environmental Protection Agency**
**Office of Inspector General**

12-4-0720
August 22, 2012

# At a Glance

## Why We Did This Review

The U.S. Environmental Protection Agency (EPA), Office of Inspector General, conducted this examination based upon an anonymous hotline complaint that expressed concerns associated with the publication of the *Bay Journal* by the Alliance for the Chesapeake Bay, Inc. (the recipient). The purpose of this examination was to determine whether the recipient's costs reported are reasonable, allowable, and allocable in accordance with the terms and condition of the cooperative agreements and whether results intended were achieved. EPA awarded the recipient five cooperative agreements between August 2005 and July 2010 with a total approved project cost of $3,619,049. The purpose of the agreements was to promote public education, outreach, and participation in the restoration of the Chesapeake Bay. One of the tasks under the cooperative agreements was to produce and publish the *Bay Journal*.

## Furthering EPA's Goals and Cross-Cutting Strategies

- *Protecting America's waters*
- *Enforcing environmental laws*

For further information, contact our Office of Congressional and Public Affairs at (202) 566-2391.

The full report is at:
www.epa.gov/oig/reports/2012/
20120822-12-4-0720.pdf

## *Examination of Costs Claimed Under EPA Cooperative Agreements CB-97324701 Through CB-97324705 Awarded to Alliance for the Chesapeake Bay, Inc.*

### What We Found

The recipient achieved the intended result of producing the *Bay Journal*, but did not comply with the Code of Federal Regulations (CFR)—specifically, 40 CFR Part 30 and 2 CFR Part 230—regarding procurement and financial management requirements. The recipient did not prepare and document a cost or price analysis, nor evaluate the performance of its *Bay Journal* contractor. Also, its federal financial reports are not supported by its accounting records. We questioned project costs totaling $1,357,035.

The recipient's written policies and procedures do not include necessary guidance to ensure compliance with 40 CFR Part 30. When recipients do not complete the required cost or price analysis, we have no assurance that costs are fair and reasonable. Due to noncompliance issues and procurement policy and procedure weaknesses, the recipient may not have the capability to manage current and future grant awards.

### Recommendations and Agency/Recipient Response

We recommend that the Regional Administrator, Region 3, disallow the total questioned project costs of $1,357,035 and recover $1,189,864 of federal funds paid under the cooperative agreements. We also recommend that the Regional Administrator require the recipient to improve its procurement internal controls and ensure that future federal financial reports are supported by accounting system data. Lastly, we recommend that certain special conditions be included for all active and future EPA awards to the recipient until the region determines that the recipient has met all applicable federal financial and procurement requirements.

Region 3 proposed an alternative resolution to review the costs of the contracts. We cannot accept this resolution because the region did not provide information on how it would demonstrate that the costs associated with the publication of the *Bay Journal* were fair and reasonable. The recipient stated that the facts do not support the recommendation to disallow and recover the claimed costs. The recipient agreed that it achieved the intended results of producing the *Bay Journal*.

**UNITED STATES ENVIRONMENTAL PROTECTION AGENCY**
WASHINGTON, D.C. 20460

August 22, 2012

## <u>MEMORANDUM</u>

**SUBJECT:** Examination of Costs Claimed Under EPA Cooperative Agreements
CB-97324701 Through CB-97324705 Awarded to
Alliance for the Chesapeake Bay, Inc.
Report No. 12-4-0720

**FROM:** Arthur A. Elkins, Jr.

**TO:** Shawn M. Garvin
Regional Administrator, Region 3

This is our report on the subject examination conducted by the Office of Inspector General (OIG) of the U.S. Environmental Protection Agency (EPA). This report contains findings that describe the problems the OIG has identified and corrective actions the OIG recommends. This report represents the opinion of the OIG and does not necessarily represent the final EPA position. Final determinations on matters in this report will be made by EPA managers in accordance with established audit resolution procedures.

### Action Required

In accordance with EPA Manual 2750, Chapter 3, you are required to provide us your proposed management decision for resolution of the findings contained in this reported before any formal resolution can be completed with the recipient. Your proposed decision is due in 120 days, or on December 20, 2012. To expedite the resolution process, please e-mail an electronic version of your proposed management decision to adachi.robert@epa.gov.

Your response will be posted on the OIG's public website, along with our memorandum commenting on your response. Your response should be provided as an Adobe PDF file that complies with the accessibility requirements of Section 508 of the Rehabilitation Act of 1973, as amended. The final response should not contain data that you do not want to be released to the public; if your response contains such data, you should identify the data for redaction or removal. We have no objection to the further release of this report to the public. This report will be available at http://www.epa.gov/oig.

If you or your staff have any questions regarding this report, please contact Melissa Heist, Assistant Inspector General for Audit, at (202) 566-0899 or heist.melissa@epa.gov; or Robert Adachi, Product Line Director, at (415) 947-4537 or adachi.robert@epa.gov.

Examination of Costs Claimed Under
EPA Cooperative Agreements CB-97324701 Through
CB-97324705 Awarded to Alliance for the Chesapeake Bay, Inc.

12-4-0720

# Table of Contents

## Appendices

# Introduction

## Purpose

The purpose of the examination was to determine whether the Alliance for the Chesapeake Bay, Inc. (the recipient):

- Reported costs that are reasonable, allowable, and allocable in accordance with the terms and conditions of cooperative agreements (CAs) CB-97324701 through CB-97324705.
- Achieved intended results of production and publication of the *Bay Journal*.

We conducted this examination based upon an anonymous hotline complaint that expressed concerns associated with the publication of the *Bay Journal*.

## Background

The U.S. Environmental Protection Agency (EPA), Region 3 Chesapeake Bay Program Office, awarded the recipient five CAs with a total approved project cost of $3,619,049. The purpose of the CAs was to promote public education, outreach, and participation in the restoration of the Chesapeake Bay. Under the CAs, EPA is to contribute 95 percent of all approved budget period costs incurred up to the total federal funding of $3,619,049. One of the tasks under the CAs was to produce and publish the *Bay Journal*. The *Bay Journal* is published to inform the public about issues and events that affect the Chesapeake Bay.

Table 1 provides basic information about authorized budget periods and funds awarded under each CA. Region 3 issued separate CAs for each budget period.

**Table 1: Schedule of cooperative agreements**

| Cooperative agreement | Award date | EPA share [a] | EPA in-kind share [b] | Recipient share | Total approved project costs | Budget periods |
|---|---|---|---|---|---|---|
| CB-97324701 | 8/10/2005 | $378,704 | $11,700 | $45,492 | $435,896 | 8/01/2005–1/31/2006 |
| CB-97324702 | 2/15/2006 | 772,264 | 23,400 | 41,896 | 837,560 | 2/01/2006–1/31/2007 |
| CB-97324703 | 1/26/2007 | 765,134 | 23,400 | 41,502 | 830,036 | 2/01/2007–1/31/2008 |
| CB-97324704 | 2/14/2008 | 684,954 | 15,600 | 36,871 | 737,425 | 2/01/2008–1/31/2009 |
| CB-97324705 | 2/02/2009 | 723,625 | 15,600 | 38,907 | 778,132 | 2/01/2009–1/31/2010 |
| Total | | $3,324,681 | $89,700 | $204,668 | $3,619,049 | |

Source: EPA CA award documents.

[a] EPA share is 95 percent of the approved budget period costs.
[b] The dollar value associated with providing space, supplies, etc., for recipient employees located at EPA facilities.

# Independent Auditor's Report

We examined costs claimed by the recipient of $3,602,784 covering the period August 1, 2005, to January 31, 2010. The recipient accepted responsibility for preparing its cost claim to comply with the requirements of the Code of Federal Regulations (CFR) in 40 CFR Part 30 and 2 CFR Part 230, and the terms and conditions of the CAs. Our responsibility is to express an opinion on the recipient's compliance and costs claimed based on our examination.

Our examination was conducted in accordance with the *Government Auditing Standards* issued by the Comptroller General of the United States, and the attestation standards established by the American Institute of Certified Public Accountants. We examined, on a test basis, evidence supporting the amount claimed under the CAs and performed other procedures we considered necessary under the circumstances. We believe our examination provides a reasonable basis for our opinion.

We conducted our examination from January 10 to December 19, 2011. We performed the following steps:

- Reviewed EPA project files
- Interviewed the recipient to obtain an understanding of the grants and the recipient's timekeeping, procurement, and federal financial reporting internal controls
- Verified deposits of EPA payments (drawdowns) to the recipient's bank statements from January through April 2010
- Reviewed costs claimed by recipient to obtain reasonable assurance that costs complied with the applicable federal laws and regulations and the terms and conditions
- Performed fraud detection procedures, including reviewing *Bay Journal* expenditures for transaction patterns, performing duplicate payment analysis, and reviewing board of director meeting minutes
- Determined whether the recipient met its cost-share match
- Determined whether the work specified under Task 2, *Bay Journal*, of the grant was accomplished
- Interviewed the recipient's external financial auditors and reviewed fiscal years 2005 through 2009 single audit reports to identify issues that might affect our examination

As part of obtaining reasonable assurance that the recipient's costs claimed under the CAs are free of material misstatement, we performed tests of its compliance with the requirements of 2 CFR Part 230, 40 CFR Part 30, and the terms and conditions of the grant. We also considered the recipient's internal controls over cost reporting to determine our examination procedures and to express our opinion on the costs claimed. Our consideration of internal controls would not necessarily disclose all internal control matters that might be material weaknesses. A material weakness is a significant deficiency or combination of significant deficiencies that results in more than a remote likelihood that a material misstatement will not be prevented or detected. A significant deficiency is a deficiency in internal control, or combination of control deficiencies, that adversely affects the recipient's ability to initiate, authorize, record, process, or report data reliably, in accordance with the applicable criteria or framework, such that there is more than a remote likelihood that a misstatement of the subject matter that is more than inconsequential will not be prevented or detected.

Our examination disclosed the following material weaknesses concerning the recipient's procurement internal controls and compliance with the requirements of 40 CFR Part 30 and 2 CFR Part 230:

- Procurement procedures do not comply with the federal procurement requirements in the award. See discussion on page 5 of this report.
- The recipient's financial records did not support the recipient's federal financial reports. See discussion on page 6 of this report.

As a result, we questioned total costs of $1,357,035 (federal share $1,289,183) of the amount claimed of $3,602,784 (federal share $3,422,645) under the CAs and recommend that EPA recover $1,189,864.

In our opinion, the costs claimed do not meet, in all material respects, the requirements of EPA Procurement Standards 40 CFR 30.45, 40 CFR 30.47, and 2 CFR Part 230, and the terms and conditions of the CAs for the project period ended January 31, 2010.

Robert K. Adachi
Director for Forensic Audits
August 22, 2012

# Results of Examination

Although the recipient achieved the intended results of producing the *Bay Journal*, the recipient did not comply with the procurement and financial management requirements specified by 40 CFR Part 30 and 2 CFR Part 230. In particular, the recipient did not:

- Prepare and document a cost or price analysis for the contract awarded to produce the *Bay Journal*
- Document how it evaluated the performance of the *Bay Journal* contractor
- Prepare federal financial reports supported by its accounting records

As a result, we question costs of $1,357,035, and EPA should recover $1,189,864 of federal funds paid under the CAs. These issues also indicate that the recipient may not have the capability to manage other current and future EPA awards.

**Table 2: Summary of claimed and questioned costs**

| Cooperative agreement | Amount claimed | Amount questioned Ineligible[a] | Unsupported[b] | Total questioned |
|---|---|---|---|---|
| CB-97324701 | $435,896 | $ 123,802 | $ 18,504 | $ 142,306 |
| CB-97324702 | 836,512 | 241,722 | 13,931 | 255,653 |
| CB-97324703 | 830,825 | 275,975 | 24,921 | 300,896 |
| CB-97324704 | 722,430 | 285,596 | 18,965 | 304,561 |
| CB-97324705 | 777,121 | 322,670 | 30,949 | 353,619 |
| Total cost | 3,602,784 | 1,249,765 | 107,270 | 1,357,035 |
| Federal share (95%) | 3,422,645 | 1,187,277 | 101,907 | 1,289,183 |
| Less net questioned costs (95%) | 1,289,183 | | | |
| Net costs (95%) | 2,133,462 | | | |
| EPA payment | 3,323,326 | | | |
| **Amount EPA should recover** | **$1,189,864** | | | |

Sources: Amounts claimed were from data the grantee provided in supporting its financial status reports/federal financial report amounts. Costs questioned based on the Office of Inspector General's (OIG's) analysis of the data.

[a] Represents contractual costs that did not comply with federal procurement requirements. See "Procurement Management Weaknesses Identified" for details.
[b] Represents costs that could not be supported by the recipient's financial records. See "Recipient's Financial Records Did Not Support Its Federal Financial Reports" for details.

## Publication of the *Bay Journal* Achieved

The CAs require the recipient to produce and publish the *Bay Journal*. EPA provided funds to inform the public about issues and events that affect the Chesapeake Bay. The recipient achieved this intended result of the CAs.

# Procurement Management Weaknesses Identified

We question ineligible costs of $1,249,765 for contractual costs associated with the *Bay Journal* because the recipient did not comply with the federal procurement requirements in the award. In particular, the recipient did not:

- Prepare and document a cost or price analysis as required under 40 CFR 30.45
- Document how it evaluated the performance of the *Bay Journal* contractor as required under 40 CFR 30.47

When the recipient applied for federal assistance, it certified that it would comply with applicable requirements of federal laws, executive orders, regulations, and policies governing each grant. The recipient did not comply with these requirements because its written policies and procurement procedures provided inadequate guidance for documenting cost or price analysis and evaluating contractor performance.

When recipients do not complete the required cost or price analysis, we have no assurance that prices are fair and reasonable.

## *Lack of Cost or Price Analysis*

We found no evidence of a cost or price analysis within the recipient's procurement files for the professional services contract awarded to produce the *Bay Journal* under Task 2 of the CAs. Title 40 CFR 30.45 requires the recipient to complete and document some form of cost or price analysis in the procurement files in connection with every procurement action.

The recipient stated that a cost or price analysis was not performed because the contractor was involved in the application and budgeting process. Simply establishing a budget and application is not a cost or price analysis as defined by 40 CFR 30.45. While a budget may provide the cost of the project on an element-by-element basis, it does not provide a review or evaluation of each element of costs for reasonableness, allocability, or allowability. Without a cost or price analysis, we have no assurance that a fair and reasonable price was obtained. Therefore, we questioned $1,249,765 claimed under the CAs. See table 2 for a summary of questioned costs by CA.

## *Lack of Evaluation of Contractor Performance*

The recipient did not evaluate the performance of the *Bay Journal* contractor to ensure compliance with the terms and conditions of the agreement, or the procurement requirements under 40 CFR 30.47. This regulation requires that the recipient maintain a system for contract administration to ensure contractor conformance with terms, conditions, and specifications of the contract. Recipients shall evaluate contractor performance and document, as appropriate, whether contractors have met the terms, conditions, and specifications of the contract. The recipient has a procurement policy and procedures for evaluating contractor performance; however, it has not documented whether the contractor has met the terms, conditions, and specifications of the contract. Without documentation demonstrating how the recipient evaluated the *Bay Journal* contractor's performance, we cannot determine whether the contractor's procurement of goods and services was proper.

## Recipient's Financial Records Did Not Support Its Federal Financial Reports

The recipient's financial records do not support the federal financial reports as required under 40 CFR 30.21(b) and 40 CFR 30.23(a). The recipient claimed costs in excess of the amount incurred. The recipient also could not support its in-kind costs.

As required by 40 CFR 30.21(b), recipients' financial management systems shall provide for the following:

1. Accurate, current, and complete disclosure of the financial results of each federally sponsored project or program in accordance with the reporting requirements set forth in 40 CFR 30.52
2. Records that identify adequately the source and application of funds for federally sponsored activities

The recipient reported total costs of $3,602,784 for the period ended January 31, 2010. However, the recipient was only able to provide accounting records supporting $3,579,588 of incurred costs under the CAs. As a result, the difference of $23,196 is unsupported. In addition, the recipient's records do not support $84,074 of in-kind costs claimed as required by 40 CFR 30.23(a), which requires all contributions to be verifiable. Accordingly we question $107,270 as unsupported. See the OIG response on page 8 for further explanation.

## Recommendations

We recommend that the Regional Administrator, Region 3:

1. Disallow the total questioned costs of $1,357,035 claimed under the CAs.

2. Recover $1,189,864 of federal funds paid in excess of the amounts determined to be allowable under the CAs.

3. Require the recipient to improve its procurement process to:

    a. Ensure compliance with 40 CFR 30.45 by conducting and documenting its cost or price analysis.

    b. Maintain documentation in its procurement files to justify sole-source procurements to ensure compliance with 40 CFR 30.46.

    c. Establish a system of contract administration to ensure contractor conformance with the terms, conditions, and specifications of the contract, and to ensure adequate and timely follow-up of all purchases, to comply with 40 CFR 30.47.

    d. Establish procedures to evaluate contractor performance and document whether contractors have met the terms and conditions of their contracts, to ensure compliance with 40 CFR 30.47.

4. Require the recipient to amend its administrative policies and procedures to document its process for preparing federal financial reports and require maintenance of data used in preparing reports to ensure compliance with 40 CFR 30.21(b).

5. Require that the following special conditions be included for all active and future EPA awards to the recipient until the region determines that the recipient has met all applicable federal financial and procurement requirements:

    a. Payment on a reimbursement basis.

    b. Review and approval by the EPA project officer of reimbursement requests, including all supporting documentation for the claims, prior to payment.

## Agency and Recipient Comments

The region did not comment on the report recommendations. It acknowledged that the recipient achieved the task of production and publication of the *Bay Journal*. The region plans to resolve the questioned project costs by researching whether the costs of the contract were fair and reasonable and disallow those costs that exceed what is allowable based on the results of its review.

The recipient stated that the facts do not support the recommendation to disallow and recover the claimed costs under the CAs. However, they agreed with our conclusion that it achieved the intended results of producing the *Bay Journal*. The recipient believed that the use and selection of its contractor complied with federal regulations. The recipient stated the use of the sole-source contractor was fully justified, documented, and disclosed to EPA in its proposal for the grant. EPA accepted the proposal based on the sole-source award and was satisfied with the performance of the contractor. Additionally, the recipient believes its continual monitoring and the successful performance of the *Bay Journal* contractor demonstrated there was no need to invest time and resources in a separate evaluation of the contractor. The recipient understands that its policies and procedures should be updated to clearly articulate language consistent with the provisions of federal procurement standards.

## OIG Response

The region proposed an alternative resolution position of reviewing the contract costs to determine whether they are fair and reasonable. We cannot accept this resolution because the region did not provide information on how it would demonstrate that the costs associated with the publication of the *Bay Journal* were fair and reasonable. As the recipient did not conduct and document a unique cost or price analysis for the selection and use of the *Bay Journal* contractor, no documentation exists to support the reasonableness of costs. Without such documentation, we cannot support the Agency's position.

Based on the recipient's comments, we have not changed our position on the costs and continue to question as ineligible costs of $1,249,765 to produce the *Bay Journal*. The recipient has not demonstrated that the production costs are reasonable, allocable, and allowable as required by 40 CFR 30.45. The recipient acknowledges it will amend its procurement policies and procedures to ensure compliance with 40 CFR Part 30.

Based on recipient information provided in response to the draft report, we eliminated the statement that the recipient did not document its justification of a noncompetitive award. Although the recipient disclosed the use of its contractor, justifying its basis for contractor selection in its February 2006 memorandum, it did not make this document available at the time of our field work. Further, this justification does not document how the contractor's costs were determined to be reasonable, allocable, and allowable.

The recipient also provided supplemental in-kind cost documentation not provided during our field work. We adjusted the unsupported questioned costs based upon the supplemental cost data. However, the recipient was still unable to support its claimed costs for the two of the CAs, as follows:

| Cooperative Agreement | Total Costs Claimed | Total Recorded Costs | Unsupported Costs |
|---|---|---|---|
| CB-97324703 | $830,825 | $810,876 | $19,949 |
| CB-97324705 | 777,121 | 773,874 | 3,247 |
| Total | | | $23,196 |

Source: Financial reports submitted to EPA and recipient's financial records.

The recipient's records provided in its response do not support its in-kind costs claimed for donated services as required by 40 CFR 30.23(a), which requires all contributions to be verifiable. The recipient incurred $205,446 of donated time by the Citizen Action Committee for its quarterly member meetings and various executive committee conference calls along with in-kind funding contributions for producing the *Bay Journal*. Based upon its conference agenda and meeting minutes, the recipient could support $82,369. As a result, the difference of $123,077 is unsupported and questioned. However, after review of the recipient's response, we have off-set the questioned cost by $39,003, representing additional allowable costs incurred but not claimed by the recipient. As a result, $84,074 is being questioned.

The full text of the region's and recipient's comments and the OIG's detailed response are included in appendices A and B of this report.

# *Status of Recommendations and Potential Monetary Benefits*

| | | RECOMMENDATIONS | | | | POTENTIAL MONETARY BENEFITS (in $000s) | |
|---|---|---|---|---|---|---|---|
| Rec. No. | Page No. | Subject | Status[1] | Action Official | Planned Completion Date | Claimed Amount | Agreed To Amount |
| 1 | 6 | Disallow the total questioned costs of $1,357,035 claimed under the CAs. | U | Regional Administrator, Region 3 | | | |
| 2 | 6 | Recover $1,189,864 of federal funds paid in excess of the amounts determined to be allowable under the CAs. | U | Regional Administrator, Region 3 | | $1,190 | |
| 3 | 7 | Require the recipient to improve its procurement process to: | | Regional Administrator, Region 3 | | | |
| | | a. Ensure compliance with 40 CFR 30.45 by conducting and documenting its cost or price analysis. | U | | | | |
| | | b. Maintain documentation in its procurement files to justify sole-source procurements to ensure compliance with 40 CFR 30.46. | U | | | | |
| | | c. Establish a system of contract administration to ensure contractor conformance with the terms, conditions, and specifications of the contract, and to ensure adequate and timely follow-up of all purchases, to comply with 40 CFR 30.47. | U | | | | |
| | | d. Establish procedures to evaluate contractor performance and document whether contractors have met the terms and conditions of their contracts, to ensure compliance with 40 CFR 30.47. | U | | | | |
| 4 | 7 | Require the recipient to amend its administrative policies and procedures to document its process for preparing federal financial reports and require maintenance of data used in preparing reports to ensure compliance with 40 CFR 30.21(b). | U | Regional Administrator, Region 3 | | | |
| 5 | 7 | Require that the following special conditions be included for all active and future EPA awards to the recipient until the region determines that the recipient has met all applicable federal financial and procurement requirements: | | Regional Administrator, Region 3 | | | |
| | | a. Payment on a reimbursement basis. | U | | | | |
| | | b. Review and approval by the EPA project officer of reimbursement requests, including all supporting documentation for the claims, prior to payment. | U | | | | |

[1] O = recommendation is open with agreed-to corrective actions pending
C = recommendation is closed with all agreed-to actions completed
U = recommendation is unresolved with resolution efforts in progress

# Agency's Comments on Draft Report and OIG Evaluation

**UNITED STATES ENVIRONMENTAL PROTECTION AGENCY**
**REGION III**
**1650 Arch Street**
**Philadelphia, Pennsylvania 19103-2029**

FEB 0 7 2012

**MEMORANDUM**

**SUBJECT:**   Response to Draft Attestation Report:
Examination of Costs Claimed Under EPA Cooperative Agreements
CB-97324701 Through CB-97324705
Awarded to Alliance for the Chesapeake Bay, Inc.
Project No. OA-FYII-A-0059

**FROM:**   James W. Newsom
Assistant Regional Administrator
Region III

**TO:**   Robert Adachi, Director of Forensic Audits
Office of Inspector General

This is response to your memorandum to Regional Administrator Shawn Garvin dated December 19, 20.11, requesting a response from Region III on the above subject draft audit attestation report for two cooperative agreements awarded to Alliance for the Chesapeake Bay (ACB). I am responding for RA Garvin as the designated Region III Audit Action Official. Thank you for providing us with the opportunity to review and comment on the draft report examining the costs claimed under these cooperative agreements.

Proper grants management, either by the recipient or by our staff, is of paramount importance to me. In that regard, I am very concerned about the findings and recommendations reached in the draft report. While the report acknowledges that the recipient achieved the task of production and publication of the Bay Journal, it recommends that the Region disallow all contractual costs associated with the journal due to noncompliance with contracting requirements. We look forward to resolving this matter by researching whether the costs of the contract were fair and reasonable and disallowing any costs over that which is allowable based on the results of our review.

Further, in the transmittal memorandum, you specifically request comments regarding the factual accuracy of the report. The only comment I have to offer on the factual nature is in regards to the statement made about the cost or price analysis by the recipient on the Bay Journal contract. In the report, it states that,

> "Title 40 CFR 30.45 requires the grantee to complete and document a cost or price analysis in the procurement files in connection with every procurement action."

Title 40 CFR 30.45 actually requires the grantee to conduct some form of a price and cost analysis in connection with every procurement action. Therefore, if ACB conducted a price or a cost analysis, then it has fulfilled the requirement of the regulation.

Again, I thank you for the opportunity to provide feedback on this report and commend you and your staff for providing a thorough review of these cooperative agreements ensuring the integrity of the taxpayers' money.

If you have any questions regarding my response, please contact Lorraine Fleury, Region III Audit Followup Coordinator at (215) 814-2341 or fleury.lorraine@epa.gov.

---

**OIG Response 1:** We concur with the region's statement that 40 CFR 30.45 requires the recipient to conduct some form of a cost or price analysis. The region plans to resolve this matter by researching whether the costs of the contracts were fair and reasonable, and then disallowing any costs over that which are allowable based on the results of its review. We cannot accept this resolution because the region did not provide information on how it would demonstrate that the costs associated with the publication of the *Bay Journal* are fair and reasonable. As the recipient did not conduct and document a unique cost or price analysis for the selection and use of the *Bay Journal* contractor, no documentation exists to support the reasonableness of costs. Without such documentation, we cannot support the Agency's position.

# Recipient's Comments on Draft Report and OIG Evaluation

February 1, 2012

Mr. Robert Adachi
Director of Forensic Audits
U.S. Environmental Protection Agency
Office of Inspector General
5 Post Office Square, Suite 100 (OID 15-1)
Boston, Massachusetts 02109-3912

Dear Mr. Adachi:

On December 19, 2011, Ms. Jean Bloom presented my office with a Draft Attestation Report entitled, *"Examination of Costs Claimed Under EPA Cooperative Agreements CB-97324701 Through CB 97324705 Awarded to Alliance for the Chesapeake Bay, Inc."* The Report presents the findings of an audit conducted by your office from December 2010 to January 2011 to evaluate five consecutive cooperative agreements (CAs) awarded through the EPA Region 3 Chesapeake Bay Program Office. The purpose of these CAs was to promote public education, outreach, and participation in the restoration of the Chesapeake Bay. One of the tasks under the CAs was to produce and publish the *Bay Journal*. The Alliance for the Chesapeake Bay (the Alliance) appreciates the opportunity to respond to this draft report, to provide information and comment on the findings made, as well as to bring to your attention information that was not included in the report, that we feel was factually inaccurate, or that should be considered by the OIG in making its final recommendations.

The Draft OIG Report contains three primary categories of results. First, the grantee's achievement of the intended results related to production of the *Bay Journal*; second, the identification of alleged material weaknesses in Procurement Management; and third, unexplained variances in financial documentation. We believe there is critical information about this grant award and the cooperative agreements that you have not requested or seen and/or is inconsistent with the conclusions in the Draft OIG Report.

501 6th Street
Annapolis, MD 21403
PH: 443-949-0575
FAX 443-949-0673

3310 Market Street, Suite A
Camp Hill, PA 17011
PH: 717-737-8622
FAX 717-737-8650
www.allianceforthebay.org

530 E. Main Street, Suite 200
Richmond, VA 23219
PH: 804-775-0951
FAX 804-775-0954

The salient facts, discussed in more detail in the attached response and attachments, are as follows:

- The Draft OIG Report confirms that the Alliance delivered all intended results of the grant with regard to quantity and quality of production of the *Bay Journal* in each of the five years in question at the cost promised and successfully achieved the objectives of informing the public about issues and events that affect the Chesapeake Bay. (Draft OIG Report, page 5 & 6)

- The Alliance was the incumbent grantee for producing the *Bay Journal* between 2000 and 2005, and contracted with Mr. Karl Blankenship as editor during that period on a sole source basis (Attachment A). All costs of that contract were accepted as reasonable and allowable. After a competitive bid process in 2010, the EPA also awarded a new 5-year grant to Mr. Karl Blankenship in 2011, who continues to produce the *Bay Journal* today (Attachment F).

- Contrary to the finding stated in the Draft OIG Report that there was "no evidence that [the Alliance] documented its justification of a noncompetitive award until February 2009," (Draft OIG Report page 5) the Alliance first documented the basis of its noncompetition award to Mr. Blankenship in February 2006 as per its procurement guidance as part of the first CA of this grant award. (Attachment B)

- Contrary to the finding that the grantee's written policies and procedures "did not include requirements for documented cost or price analysis, documenting sole-source justifications…" (Draft OIG Report page 6), the Alliance had procurement standards in place prior to the CAs in question (Attachment H).

- The Alliance's 2005 proposal includes unambiguous statements about its intent to maintain its contractual relationship with Mr. Blankenship as editor of the *Bay Journal*, without any indication of intent to compete this role (Attachment A). The EPA awarded the grant to the Alliance, at least in part, based on the Alliance's disclosed agreement to award a contract to Mr. Blankenship if the Alliance was selected for the award.

- In updated Scope of Work documents filed by The Alliance after performance of the grant was underway, the Alliance consistently stated that it would continue to contract with Mr. Blankenship in his role as editor of the *Bay Journal*. (Attachment D)

- The Alliance provided continual oversight and review of *Bay Journal* budgets and itemized expenses and Mr. Blankenship's performance and his reimbursement for costs were regularly reviewed as normal business procedure. Submission of annual CAs necessitated a review of prior performance as well as reasonableness of planned expenses for delivery of the *Bay Journal*.

- The Alliance's costs associated with the *Bay Journal* between 2005 and 2010 were roughly equivalent to the costs that the EPA had allowed under the prior 5-year grant to do the same work between 2000 and 2005 (Attachment E).

- The OIG's examination and assessment of financial records included a number of oversights or misinterpretations of the Alliance's accounting systems and records. The claim that $87,467 in costs are unsupported is not accurate and, in fact, the Alliance was underpaid for performance of the CAs. (Attachments L through P).

The attached narrative response and attachments further elaborate and document these facts for the record. Thank you for the opportunity to provide these comments.

Sincerely,


**ALBERT H. TODD**
Executive Director

cc: Jean Bloom, EPA OIG

The Draft OIG Report presents the findings of an audit conducted by the EPA OIG from December 2010 to January 2011 which evaluated five consecutive cooperative agreements (CAs) awarded to the Alliance for the Chesapeake Bay through the EPA Region 3 Chesapeake Bay Program Office. The purpose of these CAs was to promote public education, outreach, and participation in the restoration of the Chesapeake Bay. One of the tasks under the CAs was to produce and publish the *Bay Journal*.

The Draft OIG Report contains three primary categories of results. First, the grantee's achievement of the intended results related to production of the *Bay Journal*; second, the identification of alleged material weaknesses in Procurement Management; and third, unexplained variances in financial documentation. There is critical information about this grant award and the cooperative agreements that the OIG may not have requested or seen and that is inconsistent with the conclusions in the draft report.

**Overview of Pertinent Findings**

First, it should be noted that the Draft OIG Report points out that the Alliance delivered all intended results with regard to quantity and quality of *Bay Journal* production in each of the five years in question and successfully achieved the objectives of informing the public about issues and events that affect the Chesapeake Bay. These objectives were met within a budget level expected by the EPA and at the cost promised in the grant and subsequent CAs (Draft OIG Report, pages 5 & 6).

In terms of procurement process and financial documentation, in essence, the draft audit report asserts that the Alliance awarded a sole source contract under the EPA grant at issue without the kind of written justification required by the relevant regulations. The Draft OIG Report concludes that because of that alleged failure, **_all_** of the costs paid to the contractor should be disallowed. In fact, as demonstrated below, the sole-source contract at issue was fully justified and documented, the Alliance's intention to make that sole-source award was disclosed to EPA in the proposal for the grant, EPA accepted the proposal based on the sole-source award, and EPA was completely satisfied with the performance of the contractor. Regardless of the clear communication of the Alliance's intentions, the use of Mr. Blankenship as a sole source was documented with a note to the file according to Alliance Procurement guidance in both 2006 and 2009 (Attachment B).

Even if the Alliance had failed to justify the sole-source decision as required by the regulation, we understand that the appropriate remedy would be to disallow the excess cost, if any existed, paid to the contractor as a result of the lack of competition, rather than to disallow the entire cost of the contract. The evidence demonstrates that the sole-source award could not have resulted in an unreasonable or excessive payment that could have created justification for any disallowance let alone the full disallowance proposed in the Draft OIG Report. The government knew about the sole-source contract from the time it accepted the proposal, approved of the Alliance's cooperative agreements, and received the full value of the products that it paid for.

The Alliance understands that even though it has written policies and procurement procedures, they should be updated so as to clearly articulate language consistent with the provisions of 40 CFR Part 30, and the Alliance is committed to achieving those improvements within the coming months. However, we do not believe that the drastic action recommended in the report – disallowance of all costs of the contract – is justified on this premise.

In addition, the Alliance has reviewed the documentation provided by the Draft OIG Report and additional information provided on 1/18/2012, by Mr. Richard Valliere (Attachment J) related to the claims of an unexplained variance of $87,467 in the financial report. Our examination, done by staff who had no relationship to the original recording, shows that there are no unsupported expenses for the *Bay Journal*. Instead, the review showed that the Alliance could instead claim additional costs.

## DRAFT PROCUREMENT MANAGEMENT WEAKNESSES IDENTIFIED

### Background

Prior to securing the subject five-year grant in 2005, the Alliance was the incumbent grantee from August 2000 through July 2005 for work that included preparation and publishing of the *Bay Journal*. At all times during this performance period, Karl Blankenship was the editor of the *Bay Journal*—a role he has performed continuously since 1991 (Attachment A at page 1 - 5). Mr. Blankenship has won numerous awards in this capacity, including the Renewable Natural Resources Foundation's first-ever award for Excellence in Journalism in 2001 (Attachment A at page 10). Karl Blankenship's 20+ year tenure as editor of the *Bay Journal* continues today, making it hard to dispute his uniquely qualifications. In 2011, Mr. Blankenship (through his newly established business, Chesapeake Media Services, Inc.) received a new 5 year contract from the EPA to produce the *Bay Journal*.

Between August 2000 and July 2005, the Alliance received $3,680,677 in cooperative agreement grant funds under a prior grant (Attachment A at page 5). This figure is slightly more than the $3,619,049 amount for which the Alliance sought reimbursement for performing the same services during the grant at issue in your audit report, covering the period August 2005 – July 2010 (*Compare* Draft OIG Report at 1 *with* Attachment A at 5). Moreover, $1,051,459 of the $3.68 million under the prior grant was devoted to the *Bay Journal* task, compared to $1,337,232 of the $3.62 million for the grant that is the subject of your audit report. We understand that the past does not dictate the future but believe that if the Alliance's past costs or performance for the same work had been considered unsatisfactory, it is unlikely that the EPA would have agreed to continue in a similar arrangement for five more years.

The EPA was fully aware of the Alliance's long-standing contract with Mr. Blankenship and coordinated directly with Mr. Blankenship to assist in preparation of budgets and resolution of issues during the Alliance's work on the *Bay Journal*. It should also be noted that an EPA contracting officer, was in direct contact with Karl Blankenship when needed to discuss and address various budgeting issues, demonstrating that the EPA was specifically aware of Mr. Blankenship's role and had direct contact with him regarding oversight of his budget. (Attachment C at page 1 *("I have spoken to Carl [sic] to let him know that his budget should only be for what he will use between Feb and July.")*

Furthermore, it is clear from contacts with Mr. Blankenship that the EPA was aware that Mr. Blankenship was *not* an employee of the Alliance, and was thus an independent contractor. Given its experience with earlier cooperative agreements, the Alliance reasonably relied on this understanding to believe that its documentation supporting the agreement and contract was fully acceptable.

**The Alliance's 2005 Proposal**

RFP No. EPA.R3CBP-05-03 was issued in early 2005 seeking grantees for an array of tasks associated with support of the Chesapeake Bay Program. When The Alliance submitted its proposal for some of the tasks in question – including continued production of the *Bay Journal* – the Alliance clearly disclosed the fact that Mr. Blankenship had **already** been contracted to retain his role as the editor of the *Bay Journal* if an award was made to The Alliance. Within a brief eight-page proposal, there are at least five (5) clear references to Mr. Blankenship's intended role as the editor and manager of the *Bay Journal* and justify the use of his unique experience and expertise.

On the cover page of the proposal, it states:

> **"The Alliance will continue to utilize the skills of Karl Blankenship as editor of the *Bay Journal*** and of Kathleen Gaskell as layout artist. Since 1991, Mr. Blankenship has served as editor, and helped to develop the *Bay Journal* as the prime mechanism for reporting policy and science issues related to the Chesapeake Bay for the interested public. During that time, he has developed a strong working relationship not only with various Bay Program committees and subcommittees, but also with state and federal agencies, scientists, and stakeholder groups involved with the Chesapeake." (Attachment A at page 1 -emphasis added).

Under the "Background Information" section, it states:

> **"The Alliance will continue to utilize the skills of Karl Blankenship as editor of the *Bay Journal*** . . . . Since 1991, Mr. Blankenship has served as editor, and helped to develop the *Bay Journal* as the prime mechanism for reporting policy and science issues related to the Chesapeake Bay for the interested public. During that time, he has developed a strong working relationship not only with various Bay Program committees and subcommittees, but also with state and federal agencies, scientists, and stakeholder groups involved with the Chesapeake. His work with the *Bay Journal* has resulted in numerous awards including the 2001 Excellence in Journalism Award from the Renewable Natural Resources Foundation, a coalition of 14 scientific and conservation organizations. Other awards include the June Sekoll Media Award from the Maryland Department of Environment, and the Salute to

Excellence [Award] from the Maryland Governor, both in 1992. In 2003, he was a finalist for a Pew Fellowship in Marine Conservation." (Attachment A at page 2 - emphasis added).

Under the "Evaluation Criteria" section, it states:

2. Organizational Capabilities
The Alliance has assembled a team of highly qualified professionals who will form the backbone of the workforce of this project. **The Alliance for the Chesapeake Bay has a 5-year agreement to work with Karl Blankenship to produce the *Bay Journal...***

4. Ecosystem Knowledge
The Alliance's depth of knowledge is fairly extensive. **Karl Blankenship has more than 16 years of experience** in covering the Bay Program, and attending meetings, conferences, scientific gatherings, public hearings and other events related to the Bay Program and Chesapeake restoration efforts in general. He has extensive knowledge of the scientific and policy basis for restoration programs for the Bay and its watershed, from the role of riparian forest buffers and cover crops in protecting habitats and waterways to the impacts of nutrient and sediment pollution on water quality and aquatic habitat. He has extensive knowledge of the Chesapeake Bay water quality criteria, Total Maximum Daily Loads, best management practices, and the full array of laws, policies and programs that impact the bay. . . .

5. Tools and Techniques
In the past 16 years, **Karl Blankenship has had contact with a wide range of stakeholders** from watermen to watershed groups to scientists to policy makers and others involved in the Bay restoration effort.
(Attachment A at page 8 -emphasis added).

In addition to these references, the Alliance also included a full bio for Mr. Blankenship as one of the three attachments to its proposal. (Attachment A at page 10 -Proposal Attachment #2). It is clearly stated that there was no one else with the same level of experience, knowledge, acclaim, and subject-matter expertise to serve as the editor of the *Bay Journal*. We believe that the lengthy and detailed discussion of Mr. Blankenship's unique qualifications serves as the sole source justification required by the Alliance procurement guidelines and is the functional equivalent of what is called for in 40 CFR § 30.46.

Clearly, the Alliance believed that the content of the proposal itself, included in the files, satisfied the sole-source justification required and understood that EPA's acceptance of the Alliance's proposal -- including the clear indication that the Alliance would *not* compete the role of editor of the *Bay Journal* – would be tantamount to acceptance of the Alliance's sole-source justification. The only issue raised is compliance with a general regulatory requirement to justify sole source awards which the Draft OIG Report seems to suggest must be made in a different, separate document. We agree that in 2005, the Alliance could have prepared a separate document that reiterated the points made in the proposal and labeled it "Sole Source Justification" even though regulations do not clearly specify that a separate document justifying the award is required in all circumstances. However, if a separate justification were required, that document was prepared in 2006, shortly after award and again in 2009. (Attachment B).

Given these facts and their context alone, we trust that you will reconsider your recommendations.

---

**OIG Response 2**: Although the recipient disclosed the use of a contractor to the region, it is still required to follow 40 CFR 30.45 demonstrating that it evaluated the costs to determine reasonableness, allocability, and allowability. Its February 2006 sole-source justification stated, "The cost to establish this writing and editing our Bay Journal [sic] would be prohibitive and would surely lead to an interruption in our work schedule. . . ." It did not provide evidence that a cost or price review was performed. The fact that EPA approved the use of the contractor does not ensure that costs are reasonable, allocable, and allowable. The recipient must demonstrate the reasonableness of the cost of the services as required by 40 CFR 30.45. The recipient has not provided evidence to support that the costs are reasonable.

---

## The Grant Application

After receiving notice of award from the EPA, the Alliance submitted its grant application as directed in a timely fashion. In the application, the Alliance continued to be forthright about its intent to continue its existing contractual relationship with Mr. Blankenship in his role as editor of the *Bay Journal*:

> "The Alliance is requesting $130,000 to produce five issues of the *Bay Journal*. The *Bay Journal* serves as the principle public information tool of the Chesapeake Bay Program. . . . The Alliance will be responsible for development of story ideas, research, writing, editing and preparation of camera ready copy, including photographs and graphics, printing, postage, mailing list maintenance, mailing and bulk distribution to libraries. . . . **Karl Blankenship will continue to be under contract as editor of the Bay Journal**." (Attachment G - June 2005 grant request page 2 – emphasis added). An equivalent notice was included in every successive round of grant applications through 2010. The Alliance can provide further examples if requested.

The Alliance Procurement Guidelines allow for the use of sole source contracts where highly specialized knowledge or experience is required or no other sources are available. The reasons for use of a sole source are to be documented in the terms of the contract decision and the guidance calls for the funding agency to be notified (Attachment H at page 3). It is our opinion that the Alliance's Executive Director at the time, David Bancroft, would have felt that these requirements had been met by the documentation referenced in detail above. However, within 6 months of commencing performance on the first CA under this grant, the Alliance's Executive Director did issue a memo to file titled "Sole Source Justification-Karl Blankenship." It reads:

> "Mr. Blankenship is uniquely qualified to manage editing of the Bay Journal
>   because:

- He has long-time relationships with [the Alliance] and knowledge of our mission and priorities.

- The cost to establish this writing and editing of the Bay Journal would be prohibitive and would surely lead to an interruption in our work schedule during the transition to someone else, and increased costs." (Attachment B at page 1)

While the Alliance submits that its proposal alone was a sufficient sole source justification for meeting its procurement guidelines for all the reasons stated earlier, the February 2006 memo provides further evidence of the Alliance's compliance with 40 CFR § 30.46 from the first year of the Alliance's five-year performance period. Perhaps the OIG staff did not see the justification during the audit, but its existence invalidates the finding in the Draft OIG Report that states "[there is] no evidence that [the Alliance] documented its justification of a noncompetition award until February 2009." (Draft OIG Report at page 6). While The Alliance did file another sole source justification on February 2009 (Attachment B at page 2), the above-quoted memo pre-dates the memo relied on in the Draft OIG Report by three full years. Beyond these sole source memos, in each year's Scope of Work document submitted by the Alliance with its grant renewal application, it repeated that **"Karl Blankenship will continue to be under contract as editor of the Bay Journal**." (Attachment D at page 4– emphasis added). Therefore, the EPA was not only aware that the Alliance planned to continue to utilize Mr. Blankenship on a sole source basis in 2005, but that continuing intention was confirmed each year between 2005 and 2010.

> **OIG Response 3**: Based on the recipient's response, we eliminated the reference in the draft report stating that we found no evidence that the recipient documented its justification of a noncompetitive award until February 2009. Title 40 CFR 30.46 requires the grantee to document the basis for contractor selection and justification for lack of competition when competitive bids or offers are not obtained. Although the recipient disclosed the use of its contractor, justifying its basis for contractor selection in its February 2006 memorandum, it did not make this document available to us at the time of our field work. Further, this justification does not demonstrate that the contractor's costs are reasonable, allocable, and allowable.

## Documentation of Blankenship Role in Contract Performance

Alliance Procurement Guidelines state that "[the Alliance] will evaluate contractor performance and document, as appropriate, whether contractors have met the terms, conditions, and specifications of the contract. The Executive Director of the Alliance continually reviewed the quality of *Bay Journal* production on an issue by issue basis and had to approve payments on a regular basis to reimburse Mr. Blankenship for costs incurred in its production. Although not necessarily documented, payments for work on the *Bay Journal* would not have been made without a review of the costs and deliverables specifically related to the contract. In addition, through quarterly grant reports and their review, there is a continuous feedback loop on performance with EPA as the funding agency. The provision of and approval of quarterly reports are requirement of the CAs. The need to annually reapply for approval to continue this work through a new CA also mandated a regular examination by the Alliance Executive Director of the budget associated with the *Bay Journal*, and the expenses proposed for its production and delivery.

With this knowledge, the EPA continued to give the Alliance positive evaluations throughout the review process, including in the specific area of the production of the *Bay Journal*. The Draft OIG Report itself does not dispute this and concludes that The Alliance "achieved the intended result of producing the *Bay Journal*." (Draft OIG Report at page 5) and "inform the public about issues and events that affect the Chesapeake Bay." (Draft OIG Report at page 6). Accordingly, there is no dispute that Mr. Blankenship capably performed the job he was hired to do.

Relevant regulations have general requirements that grant recipients evaluate contractor performance and document, as appropriate, whether contractors have met the terms, conditions and specifications of the contract. The process of regular grant review through quarterly reports is identified as a method adequate for this purpose. Neither 40 CFR § 30.47 nor § 30.51 require a grantee to conduct a separate performance evaluation be prepared to monitor contract performance unless issues dictate the requirement of such measures.

As such, the Alliance did not conduct a separate parallel review of its *Bay Journal* contractor, outside of continual monitoring of *Bay Journal* production and quality, and quarterly review of the CA by the EPA. Based on successful performance of contracted tasks, positive feedback from the public and the EPA, and the continued on schedule production of the *Bay Journal* within established costs, the need to invest time and resources in such a separate evaluation would have served no real purpose under the circumstances and would have been duplicative of the EPA's regular evaluation of the *Bay Journal* work.

Moreover, even if it could be considered critical that the Alliance failed to prepare written evaluations of Mr. Blankenship's performance, there was no damage to the EPA from that failure and certainly no justification for disallowing any portion of the payments made to Mr. Blankenship as a contractor based on the quality of his work. It should also be noted that if the Alliance had been required to prepare written evaluations on a regular basis, the cost of their preparation should have been included as an allowable reimbursable cost in the grant. It is unlikely that these evaluations would have resulted in any change in relationships or outputs under the grant.

---

**OIG Response 4**: The recipient's own guidelines require it to evaluate contractor performance and document, as appropriate, whether contractors have met the terms, conditions, and specifications of the contract. Title 40 CFR 30.47 requires a system for contract administration to ensure contractor conformance and compliance with contractual terms where 40 CFR 30.51 makes the recipient responsible for monitoring and reporting project performance. Without a system to monitor and document contractor performance, we cannot determine whether the recipient's procurement of goods and services was adequate.

Also, a written evaluation is just one factor in determining the allowability of the costs claimed. Another factor is whether the costs are reasonable, allocable, and allowable within the terms of the CA. The recipient's response did not address the reasonableness or allowability of costs at the time of contract award.

---

## Cost or Price Analysis (Attachment I)

The Draft OIG Report states on page 5 (emphasis added) that the "grantee did not: Prepare and document a cost **_and_** price analysis for the contract awarded to the *Bay Journal*." Title 40 CFR 30.45 requires that "Some form of cost **_or_** price analysis shall be made and documented in the procurement files in connection with every procurement action. Price analysis may be accomplished in various ways, including the comparison of price quotations submitted, market prices and similar indicia, together with discounts. Cost analysis is the review and evaluation of each element of cost to determine reasonableness, allocability and allowability." (emphasis added)

Evaluation of past performance and the ability to work within budget limitations for this task under the EPA CAs was routinely reviewed during the year as discussed above and annually as new CA proposals were compiled. Although the Alliance did not conduct and document a unique cost or price analysis for the selection and use of Mr. Karl Blankenship as the editor and writer of the *Bay Journal* for the sole source reasons stated above, printing and mailing of the Bay Journal were regularly competed with various available vendors (Attachment I. For the purpose of response to this Draft OIG Report, the Alliance compiled additional cost information about the *Bay Journal* and Mr. Blankenship's role as well as a comparison of *Bay Journal* costs with the costs of other similar publications. It is our hope that this information will help to better inform the Report recommendations.

In general, comparative services provided by private sources consistently demonstrate that Mr. Blankenship continually performed at or below the prevailing market costs for services of similar complexity and quality. The fact that these costs were low and remained that way over time (when reviewed on an annual basis as part of the CA application process) is certainly cause for the decision to not perform repeated cost analysis over the period in question and why the Alliance continued to use Mr. Blankenship as its contractor. Although, writing, editing, and layout services remained with Mr. Blankenship, costs of printing and distribution were repeatedly competed to obtain the lowest and most reasonable cost possible (Attachment I).

---

**OIG Response 5**: The recipient states it did not conduct a cost or price analysis of the editor and writer of the journal because of the contractor's past performance and ability to work within budgets. In response to our report, the recipient prepared a cost analysis using actual payments to the contractor. The analysis is not based on the contractor's cost data including the contractor's direct labor and indirect costs. Instead, the analysis was based upon an industry average and included indirect cost factors that were not supported. This analysis is not a specific review and evaluation of each cost component to determine the reasonableness, allocability, and allowablity of costs. Part of the documentation presented to justify its review of printing and mailing costs is outside the CA project period. Title 40 CFR 30.45 defines a cost analysis as a review and evaluation of each element of cost to determine reasonableness, allocability, and allowability. The recipient has not provided evidence to demonstrate that the costs are reasonable, allocable, and allowable.

---

**Conclusions relevant to Procurement Management Weaknesses Identified**

The EPA awarded a five year grant and entered into successive cooperative agreements from 2005-2010 with the Alliance that included unambiguous language and justification about the Alliance's intent to issue a sole source contract to Mr. Karl Blankenship. The arrangements and the costs relevant to this grant were similar to what Mr. Blankenship had been paid under the incumbent's previous grant (2000-2005). The EPA awarded the grant to the Alliance knowing that Mr. Blankenship would reprise his role as editor. The award itself was a clear recognition that the proposed costs were reasonable in the eyes of the EPA and the continuation of funding in subsequent years is clear recognition that the EPA concurred that his work was completely in a fully satisfactory manner.

Documentation of the unique reasons for use of Mr. Blankenship as sole source contractor for the *Bay Journal* that the Alliance included in its proposals, grant applications and subsequent agreements and performance reports was suitable for meeting its procurement guidelines and additional memos to files in 2006 and 2009 reiterated its justification of this choice as required by relevant regulations. The EPA assented to the Alliance's proposal terms, approved the Alliance's contracting approach, funded the Alliance's subsequent grant application, and reaped the benefit in the form of excellent, on-budget grant performance. The Alliance respectfully submits that the facts do not support the recommendation to penalize the Alliance and request that all payments related to the CAs be refunded to the EPA six years after the fact. We hold that the Alliance did exactly what it promised to do, at the price and in the way it promised to perform.

While we understand and accept the importance of the regulatory requirements and recognize that any shortcoming in the Alliance's written policies and practices about such matters should and will be remedied, there is no reason to conclude that any failure to comply with those requirements in this particular situation caused any harm to the EPA nor would justify any disallowance at all, much less 100 percent of the amounts paid to Mr. Blankenship. To the contrary, costs for the Bay Journal as produced by Mr. Blankenship are competitive and even a bargain when compared with the production of publications of similar scope and quality. Moreover, the Draft OIG Report cites no provision in the regulations or the grant that would support disallowing the Alliance's expenses where services were fully performed on-budget and there is no allegation or documentation suggested that the work could have been performed at a lower cost or better quality by anyone else.

> **OIG Response 6**: Although the recipient disclosed the use of its contractor and according to the recipient, EPA approved the use of a contractor—this does not represent approval of the contractor's contract. The approval does not ensure that the costs are reasonable, allocable, and allowable. The recipient must demonstrate the reasonableness of the cost of the services as required by 40 CFR 30.45. The recipient has not provided such evidence. The recipient also recognizes that its written policies and procedures should and will be remedied.

**GRANTEE FINANCIAL RECORDS AND FEDERAL FINANCIAL REPORTS –
UNSUPPORTED EXPENSES**

The Draft OIG Report states that the grantee did not, "Prepare federal financial reports based upon or supported by its accounting records." The Alliance has reviewed the report and the additional documents supplied by the OIG on January 18, 2012 and carefully evaluated the methods used to arrive at the conclusions made. We have identified a variety of oversights and misinterpretations of the Alliance's accounting systems and records that we believe have led to these conclusions. The following are key findings made in this reexamination of the Report:

- The OIG's examination did not take into account the fact that the total project expenditures which are reported on line 10a on the SF269 (Attachment J) include, as required, in-kind costs that are not captured in the Alliance's accounting software. As an illustration, the total project expenditures include: the in-kind EPA contribution of office space and office equipment, volunteer time, and in one case, a private foundation matching grant.
- The actual federal share of total expenditures reported on line 10j of the SF269 (Attachment J) which represents the cash reimbursements to the Alliance by the federal government matches the total Alliance expenses that are recorded in the Alliance accounting system. The only exception to this accounting occurred with grant CB97324702 (ACB Job 26) where the federal share listed on line 10j in fact, is <u>lower</u> than the total of Alliance expenditures captured in the accounting software.
- It is also important to note that the indirect cost rates (SF 269 line 11) that were used by the Alliance in reporting and billing its costs, in all but one case, were lower than the final negotiated rates for each year. It would be allowable for the Alliance to request that additional funds be paid by the USEPA to the Alliance to account for this underpayment (Attachment J and Attachment K Indirect Cost Rate History)
- The OIG information provided to the Alliance 1/18/12 report includes one small error. For the record, Agreement # CB97324703 was Job 27 in the Alliance's accounting records, not Job 37, as listed in the OIG attachments provided 1/18/12 (Attachment J).

**Expenses:**
Outlined below are additional expenses not recognized by the OIG in their investigations, analyses, and reporting, but clearly captured by the Alliance's financial record-keeping systems, as outlined below.

| Agreement Number | ACB Job # | Total Expenses According to the OIG * | Additional In-Kind Not Included in OIG Report** | EPA In-Kind Not Included in OIG Report** | Matching Funds Not Included in OIG Report** | Total Expenses left out of OIG Report | Corrected Total Expenses |
|---|---|---|---|---|---|---|---|
| CB-97324701 | 275 | $ 401,717 | $ 8,479 | $ 11,700 | $ 14,000 | $ 34,179 | $ 435,896 |
| CB-97324702 | 26 | $ 836,650 | | $ 23,400 | | $ 23,400 | $ 860,050 |
| CB-97324703 | 27 | $ 808,113 | | $ 23,400 | | $ 23,400 | $ 831,513 |
| CB-97324704 | 28 | $ 716,045 | $ 6,250 | $ 15,600 | | $ 21,850 | $ 737,895 |
| CB-97324705 | 29 | $ 758,273 | | $ 15,600 | | $ 15,600 | $ 773,873 |
| **Totals** | | **3,520,798** | | | | **$ 118,429** | **$ 3,639,227** |

\* See Attachment J  OIG "Summary of Recorded Costs and Reported Outlays"
\*\* See Attachments  L through  P

Analysis of these expenses, taking into consideration the proper and allowable accounting for match and in-kind expenses, indicates that the Alliance, over the five year period, actually incurred more expenses related to the delivery of the Bay Journal task that it was compensated for.  The total expenditures not recognized by the OIG in its supporting documentation is $118,492.   This is supported by the documentation attached (and listed below).

**Agreement # CB97324701( Job 275)**   (Attachment L)
- Additional In-kind - $8,479 (OIG report listed $23,013 actual was $31,492
- EPA In-kind          $11,700 (reference award document )
- Keith Campbell Foundation $14,000 (match tracked under Job 335 )

**Agreement CB 97324702, (Job 26)**  (Attachment M)
- EPA In-kind          $23,400 (reference award document)

**Agreement CB 97324703, Job 27**   (Attachment N)
(listed incorrectly on OIG spreadsheet provided 1/18/12)
- EPA In-kind          $23,400 (reference award document )

**Agreement CB 97324704 (Job 28)**   (Attachment O)
- Additional In-kind     $6,250 (OIG report listed $31,570 actual was $37,820)
- EPA In-kind   $15,600 (reference award document )

**Agreement CB 97324705 (Job 29)**   (Attachment P
- EPA In-kind          $15,600 (reference award document)

The Alliance's accounting systems and federal financial reports indicate that in essence the Alliance did not request reimbursement of all expenses and in fact had expenses in excess of what was reported in performance of the *Bay Journal* task.  Our analysis indicates that all expenses for which the Alliance was compensated were fully supported. When all information is considered, the claim that $87,467 in costs is unsupported is not justified.

---

**OIG Response 7**: The recipient states that the auditor's conclusions are based on a variety of oversights and misinterpretations. We made many requests, from the date of the notification letter to the issuance of the draft report, for documentation so that we could gain an understanding of the composition of claimed costs. The recipient's staff was unable to support all sources and applications of project costs for each of the CAs under review. One reason was that the executive director, director of finance, and grants manager, who oversaw most of the CA activities, were no longer employed and had been replaced by temporary staff. Some of the temporary staff were part-time employees with little or no knowledge of financial records for the CAs. In the recipient's response, the recipient's new management still could not reconcile its claimed costs to its records. The recipient's records did contain some documentation for in-kind costs at the time of our field work, but the recipient was unable to provide supporting documentation for all of its in-kind costs.

In its response to the draft report, the recipient included supplemental in-kind cost documentation not provided during our examination. However, the recipient could not support all of its in-kind costs claimed for donated services as required by 40 CFR 30.23(a). Specifically, the recipient claimed unsupported hours for the donated services of the Citizen Action Committee in excess of its meeting agendas and minutes or conference calls, and without explanation. The recipient also claimed costs identified as additional funding contributions for the *Bay Journal* but did not provide any evidence to support these costs. We accepted the in-kind costs of providing EPA space, supplies, etc., for the recipient's staff located on-site at EPA, as required by the CA, and the $14,000 of matching funds identified under a separate project number. We have also off-set the in-kind questioned costs by additional allowable costs incurred but not reported.

The recipient stated that it used an indirect cost rate lower than its negotiated rate when preparing its costs claimed on the federal financial reports. It did not identify the under-reported indirect costs. EPA will need to determine whether the unrecovered costs can be used to off-set the questioned costs or claimed for reimbursement within the award limits.

---

## Enhancement of Alliance Financial Systems and Guidance

Although not addressed in the Draft OIG Report from the EPA OIG, since late 2010 when the audit began, the Alliance for the Chesapeake Bay has taken significant steps to improve its financial management systems and staffing and to improve accounting software. The Alliance's Executive Director hired Elizabeth Biggs in January 2011 for the expressed purpose of bringing experienced non-profit accounting expertise to its financial management systems. As of January 1, 2011, the Alliance abandoned its cumbersome accounting software package known as ACCPAC and began implementation of new *Peachtree Complete* Accounting software. In 2011, the Alliance replaced financial and bookkeeping staff who lacked sufficient expertise to fully manage a nonprofit accounting system.

In is important to note that the Alliance as a matter of financial policy segregates in-kind revenue and expense items from monetary items in its non-profit financial accounting systems. See recommendations by the "Nonprofit Overhead Project" sponsored by the Atlantic Philanthropies, The Ford Foundation, The Charles Stewart Mott Foundation, the David and Lucille Packard Foundation, and the Rockefeller Brothers Fund. The Alliance memorialized, effective January 1, 2011 the existing financial management policy and procedure on documenting in-kind contributions which includes recording:

(a) The date and location of the in-kind contribution.
(b) As appropriate, the name and signature of the donor.
(c) A description of the goods or services.
(d) The estimated fair market value of the contribution.
(e) How or who estimated the value.

Based on recommendations in the Draft OIG Report, the Alliance will also revise its 2004 Procurement Guidelines to use specific language that will better articulate the intent of 40 CFR 30 related to contracting provisions such as cost or price analysis, documentation of sole source and evaluation of performance.

**OIG Response 8**: The recipient acknowledged it will amend its procurement policies and procedures to ensure compliance with 40 CFR Part 30.

## ATTACHMENT LIST

Attachment A: 2005 Alliance for the Chesapeake Bay Proposal for EPA Grant

Attachment B: 2006 and 2009 Sole Source Justification Statements

Attachment C: Emails with EPA Grant Officer

Attachment D: 2006 CA Scope of Work

Attachment E: Alliance 2000-2005 *Bay Journal* Costs

Attachment F: *Bay Journal* Web Contact Page

Attachment G: Alliance June 2005 Grant Request

Attachment H: Alliance 2004 Procurement Standards

Attachment I: Cost Analysis for *Bay Journal* and other comparable publications

Attachment J: Information provided to the Alliance by OIG on 1/18/12

Attachment K: Alliance Indirect Cost History

Attachment L: Documentation related to Agreement # CB97324701( Job 275): Total In-kind match contributed by CAC members from 8/1/05 – 1/31/06, Award document CB-97324701-0, and Keith Campbell Foundation award letter and budget vs. actual report for Job 335

Attachment M: Documentation related to Agreement CB 97324702, (Job 26): Agreement Award document CB-97324702-0 and Amendment 1, CB-97324702-1 funding increase.

Attachment N: Award document CB-97324703

Attachment O: Documentation related to Agreement CB 97324704 (Job 28): Total In-kind match contributed by CAC members from 2/1/2008 – 1/31/2009 and Post Award Evaluation Protocol for Grant CB-97324704

Attachment P: Award document CB97324705-0 (Job 29)

# *Distribution*

Regional Administrator, Region 3
Assistant Regional Administrator, Region 3
Agency Follow-Up Official (the CFO)
Agency Follow-Up Coordinator
Director, Grants and Interagency Agreements Management Division,
      Office of Administration and Resources Management
Regional Public Affairs Officer, Region 3
Audit Follow-Up Coordinator, Region 3
Executive Director, Alliance for the Chesapeake Bay, Inc.

www.ingramcontent.com/pod-product-compliance
Lightning Source LLC
Chambersburg PA
CBHW081803280526
45789CB00008B/2985